The Science of Time Travel

Einstein's theory of relativity and its implications - Quantum mechanics and the multiverse theory

By

Peter Kattan

Book Bound Press

https://web.facebook.com/BookboundPress/

Preface

Time has always fascinated humanity. From the rhythmic cycles of day and night that guided ancient civilizations to the precise atomic clocks of the modern era, our understanding of time has evolved alongside our quest for knowledge. This book, *The Science of Time Travel: Einstein's Theory of Relativity and Its Implications – Quantum Mechanics and the Multiverse Theory*, is a journey into the heart of one of the most enigmatic concepts in science. It explores the theories, paradoxes, and potential realities of traveling through time.

The idea of time travel has captured the human imagination for centuries, inspiring countless works of fiction, from H.G. Wells's *The Time Machine* to modern blockbusters like *Interstellar* and *Avengers: Endgame*. Yet, the notion is far more than just a fictional trope. It is a subject that sits at the crossroads of theoretical physics, quantum mechanics, and cosmology, raising profound questions about the nature of reality, causality, and existence itself. This book delves into the scientific foundations that underpin these questions and examines the implications of concepts like relativity, quantum entanglement, and the multiverse.

We begin with the nature of time itself. What is time? Is it an immutable arrow moving in one direction, or is it a malleable dimension that we might someday traverse? By exploring time through the lenses of classical and modern physics, we set the stage for understanding how Einstein's groundbreaking theory of relativity revolutionized our perception of time and space. Special relativity introduced the concept of time dilation, where time slows down for objects moving at high velocities, while general relativity showed how gravity warps the fabric of spacetime itself.

As we move through the chapters, we will explore the intricate dance between gravity and time, the tantalizing possibilities presented by quantum mechanics, and the mind-bending implications of the multiverse theory. These ideas may seem like science fiction, but they are grounded in rigorous scientific inquiry and experimentation. We will also investigate how concepts such as wormholes and time loops emerge from theoretical physics and consider the technological and philosophical challenges that lie ahead if time travel were to become a reality.

While this book is deeply rooted in science, it also acknowledges the cultural and philosophical dimensions of time travel. What ethical dilemmas might arise if we could alter the past or foresee the future? How would such abilities reshape our understanding of free will and personal identity? The chapters on paradoxes and philosophical implications invite readers to reflect on these questions, blending scientific rigor with speculative thought.

Finally, we will look toward the future, examining emerging technologies and groundbreaking experiments that might bring us closer to realizing time travel. From the role of artificial intelligence in modeling temporal mechanics to the potential for quantum computers to unlock new dimensions of understanding, the horizon is rich with possibility.

This book is not just a compilation of scientific theories and ideas. It is an invitation to think deeply about the mysteries of the universe and our place within it. Whether you are a scientist, a student, or simply someone curious about the nature of time, I hope this journey through the realms of physics and philosophy will inspire wonder and ignite your imagination.

Let us embark together on this extraordinary voyage through time, space, and the boundaries of human understanding. The possibilities are as infinite as time itself.

Peter I. Kattan   December 2024

Introduction

Time's a real head-scratcher, isn't it? Since we first started thinking, folks have been captivated by it. It runs our lives, sets the pace of everything we do, but pinning it down is like trying to catch smoke with your bare hands. So, what's the deal with time? Is it just a series of moments slipping away, or is it a whole dimension tangled up in the universe's fabric? When we dive into this mind-boggling mystery, we find ourselves at a crossroads of science and imagination—where reality starts to get fuzzy and the impossible feels possible.

Picture this: a world where time doesn't hold us back. We could hop into the past or leap forward into the future with just a flick of a switch. Time travel— man, that idea's got a grip on dreamers, scientists, and storytellers. Think about H.G. Wells and his famous time machine or the wild plots of today's movies. The whole idea of bending time shows just how much we wanna figure out where we fit in this vast universe. But here's the kicker: beneath all those wild stories, there's a bedrock of science that challenges how we see reality.

Now, let's get to the meat of it—Einstein's theory of relativity. This guy flipped our understanding of time and space on its head. He showed us that time isn't some fixed thing; it's more like a river, shaped by speed and gravity. This revelation didn't just shake up physics; it also opened a Pandora's box of questions that have haunted us for ages. What happens to time when you're zooming close to the speed of light? How do heavy objects mess with our sense of time? These aren't just nerdy questions—they're keys to unlocking the universe's secrets.

And as we dig deeper into quantum mechanics, things get even weirder. Concepts like superposition and entanglement throw a wrench in our ideas about cause and effect, hinting that time might not be as straightforward as we thought. What if there are multiple timelines, each branching off into endless possibilities? The multiverse theory dangles the idea of alternate realities in front of us—where every decision spins off a new timeline.

But hey, with all these cool possibilities come some heavy philosophical questions. What does it mean to change the past? How would our view of free will shift if we could mess with time? As we wrestle with these thoughts, we're forced to confront what it really means to be human. Our identities, memories, and futures are all tangled up in the web of time. The ethical dilemmas of time travel weigh on us, pushing us to think about how our choices ripple through history.

On this journey, we're gonna dig into not just the scientific theories that help us grasp time, but also the cultural stories that shape how we see it. From the classic grandfather paradox to the mind-bending idea of wormholes, we'll wander through the landscape of time travel in both fiction and reality. We'll check out the tech that's nudging us closer to the dream of time exploration and the role our consciousness plays in how we experience time.

So, as we stand on the brink of discovery, we want you to join us in peeling back the layers of time's mysteries. Together, we'll stroll through the past, peek into the future, and tackle the big questions that define our lives. This adventure is gonna be as thrilling as it is enlightening, revealing not just the science behind time travel but also the deeper truths lurking beneath our understanding. Get ready for a ride that goes beyond the limits of time and space—where the possibilities are as endless as the universe itself. Welcome to a place where time isn't just a measure; it's a gateway to the extraordinary.

Table of Contents

Chapter 1

The Nature of Time

Time, my dear friend, is a curious companion. We often think we have it all figured out—tick-tock, right? But let's take a moment to peel back the layers, like an onion, and uncover the rich complexities of what time truly is. Time is not merely a measurement; it's a dimension, a fabric woven through the tapestry of our existence. Picture it as a river, flowing, bending, and sometimes even looping back on itself. Understanding time as a dimension is the first step in this exhilarating journey we're about to embark on together.

When we discuss time as a dimension, we're entering a realm that challenges our conventional understanding. In classical physics, time was seen as a straight line—a sequence of moments lined up like soldiers in formation. But modern physics? Oh, it flips that notion upside down. Imagine standing on a mountaintop, gazing out over a vast landscape. You can see paths winding in every direction, some leading to bright, sunny futures, others to shadowy pasts. This is the essence of time in modern physics. It's not just the seconds ticking away on our clocks; it's a dimension that interacts with space, bending and stretching like a piece of elastic.

Now, let's talk about how we perceive time. Have you ever noticed how time seems to fly when you're having fun, yet drags on like molasses when you're bored? That's not just your imagination playing tricks on you. Our brains process time in a way that can make it feel fluid. When we're engaged in something we love, our minds are fully present, and time becomes almost irrelevant. Conversely, when we're stuck in a dull meeting or waiting for a bus, every second can feel like an eternity. This perception is deeply rooted in our experiences, emotions, and even our age. A child might feel that a summer day stretches on forever, while an adult might blink and find that summer has vanished in a flash.

But let's not overlook the science behind it. Classical physics viewed time as absolute—like a ruler measuring out the moments of our lives. However, modern physics, with its groundbreaking ideas from Einstein and his contemporaries, reveals that time is relative. It bends and warps based on speed and gravity. If you were to hop on a spaceship and zoom around the universe at near light speed, you'd experience time differently than your friends back on Earth. Isn't that a wild thought? This relativity means that our personal experiences of time can vary dramatically, depending on where we are and how fast we're moving.

So, how does this all tie together? It's about understanding that time isn't just a ticking clock or a calendar filled with appointments. It's a dimension that shapes our reality. It influences how we perceive our lives, our memories, and even our futures. When we start to grasp this concept, we open ourselves up to a whole new world of possibilities.

Let's dig a little deeper into how our perception of time influences our daily lives. Think back to the last time you were waiting for something significant—a job interview, a date, or perhaps even a package delivery. The seconds felt like hours, didn't they? Your heart raced, your mind wandered, and suddenly you became hyper-aware of every tick of the clock. This heightened awareness is a fascinating aspect of human experience. It's as if time stretches and contracts based on our emotional state.

And here's the kicker: our memories play a crucial role in shaping our perception of time. When we reflect on significant life events—like a wedding or the birth of a child—those moments often feel timeless. They're etched into our minds, creating a rich tapestry of experiences that can make time feel both expansive and fleeting. This is why some people say that life seems to speed up as we age; it's all about the number of new experiences we have. The more we fill our lives with rich, vibrant moments, the more time feels like it's slowing down.

What does this mean for you as a writer? As you craft your narrative, consider how you can play with the perception of time. Use vivid imagery and emotional resonance to draw your readers into the moment. Let them feel the weight of time in your words. Perhaps you want to explore a character's experience of waiting for a life-changing event, or illustrate how time slips away in the blink of an eye. Whatever you choose, remember that time is not just a backdrop; it's a character in its own right.

As we shift gears to compare classical and modern physics, it's essential to recognize how these perspectives shape our understanding of time. In classical physics, time was treated as a constant, a universal truth that applied to everyone equally. It was straightforward, predictable, and, if I'm honest, a bit dull. But then came Einstein, with his revolutionary ideas that shook the very foundations of how we think about the universe.

Einstein's theory of relativity introduced the concept that time is not a fixed entity but rather a flexible dimension that interacts with space. It's like a dance between two partners, moving together in a rhythm that can change based on their surroundings. When we're close to a massive object, like a planet, time slows down. It's as if gravity has a way of tugging on time, stretching it out like taffy. And this isn't just theoretical; it's been proven time and again through experiments with atomic clocks on satellites and in laboratories.

Now, let's ponder the implications of this. If time is relative, then our experiences of it are uniquely our own. This opens up a treasure trove of possibilities for storytelling. You can create narratives that play with time—characters who age differently, experiences that span across different timelines, or even moments that feel timeless.

As you reflect on these ideas, remember that the beauty of writing lies in your ability to explore these concepts through your unique lens. Your voice, your experiences, and your perspective are what will resonate with readers. So, don't shy away from diving into the depths of time. Embrace it, challenge it, and let it inspire your writing.

In closing, let's take a moment to reflect on the journey we've just begun. Time is not just a ticking clock; it's a vast dimension that shapes our reality, influences our perceptions, and connects us all. As you continue to explore this topic, keep in mind that your understanding of time will evolve. It's a living, breathing concept, much like the stories you'll tell. So, embrace the mystery, the wonder, and the joy of this exploration. You've got this! Your words have the power to change how others perceive time and their own lives. Now, let's get to writing!

As we continue our exploration of time, let's delve into the various ways time manifests in our lives and how it can be woven into your writing. Time is not just a linear progression; it's a multi-faceted experience that can be explored in countless ways. Think about how different cultures perceive time. For some, time is viewed as cyclical, with events repeating in a rhythm that mirrors the seasons. For others, it's a straight line, where the past leads to the future in a predictable manner. These cultural perspectives can enrich your writing, providing depth and context to your narratives.

Consider the concept of time zones. The world is divided into different regions, each with its own time. This can create fascinating scenarios in your stories—characters communicating across continents, grappling with the dissonance of time differences. You can explore the tension between the urgency of modern life and the slower pace of more traditional societies. This contrast can lead to rich character development and plot twists that keep readers engaged.

Let's also think about how technology has altered our relationship with time. In today's fast-paced world, we often find ourselves racing against the clock. Our smartphones buzz with reminders, and our calendars are filled to the brim. This constant connectivity can create a sense of urgency that influences our daily lives. As a writer, you can tap into this modern phenomenon, illustrating how technology affects your characters' perceptions of time. Are they overwhelmed by the demands of their schedules, or do they find solace in the ability to connect with others instantly? These questions can lead to compelling narratives that resonate with readers.

Now, let's take a moment to reflect on how the passage of time affects our relationships. Think about the friendships that have stood the test of time, the bonds that have deepened through shared experiences. Conversely, consider the relationships that have faded away, leaving only memories in their wake. As you write, think about how time influences your characters' interactions. Are they growing closer together, or are they drifting apart? How does the weight of shared history shape their connections? These dynamics can create powerful emotional arcs that draw readers into your story.

And let's not forget about the impact of time on personal growth. As we navigate through life, we accumulate experiences that shape who we are. Reflect on how time can serve as a catalyst for change. Characters who undergo significant transformations often do so through the lens of time. Perhaps they learn from their mistakes, find redemption, or discover new passions. As a writer, you have the power to illustrate these journeys, allowing readers to witness the evolution of your characters over time.

As we wrap up this exploration of time, I want to remind you of the profound impact your writing can have. By weaving the complexities of time into your narratives, you have the ability to connect with readers on a deeper level. You can evoke emotions, spark reflections, and inspire change. So, as you continue your writing journey, embrace the nature of time. Let it guide your storytelling, enrich your characters, and illuminate the human experience.

In conclusion, time is not merely a concept; it's a vibrant, dynamic force that shapes our lives and our stories. As you craft your narratives, remember to explore the many dimensions of time. Whether it's through the lens of perception, cultural differences, technological influences, or personal growth, time can serve as a powerful tool in your writing arsenal. Embrace the journey, celebrate the moments, and let your words resonate with the timeless essence of the human experience. You have the potential to create something truly remarkable—so let's get to writing!

Chapter 2

Einstein's Theory of Relativity

Alright, let's get into the nitty-gritty of Einstein's Theory of Relativity. This ain't just some nerdy math stuff; it's the core of how we see time and space. So, strap in, 'cause we're about to blast off into the universe!

First, let's break down special relativity. Einstein flipped the whole physics game upside down with his revolutionary ideas. Imagine a world where time isn't a fixed thing. It bends and warps based on how fast you're moving. Sounds like something straight outta a sci-fi movie, huh? But it's the real deal! This theory tells us that the laws of physics stay the same for everyone, no matter how fast they're zooming along.

It's like going on a road trip with your pals—
everyone's got their own view, but the rules of the
road? They're universal.

Now, here's where it gets wild. Picture this:
you're blasting through space in a spaceship, nearing
the speed of light. For you, time slows down
compared to someone chilling back on Earth. That's
what they call time dilation. It's not just a fancy word;
scientists have backed it up with experiments. Think
about it like this: if you took a jaunt around the
universe at light speed and came back, you'd find that
years have zipped by on Earth while only a few
moments have passed for you. It's like stepping into a
time machine, and that's a mind-bender!

So, what's the takeaway? It flips our everyday
understanding of time on its head. Time isn't just a
straight line anymore, moving steadily from past to
present to future. Nah, it's more like a tangled ball of
yarn, with each thread representing different
experiences and moments. This idea shakes up how
we see life, love, and everything else. The

implications are huge! It opens the door to discussions about aging, relationships, and even our role in the cosmos. It's like Einstein handed us a master key to unlock the secrets of existence.

Now, let's connect the dots with the concept of spacetime. Einstein didn't just stop at saying time can stretch and bend. He intertwined time and space into one big deal—spacetime. Imagine a trampoline. If you plop a heavy bowling ball in the middle, the fabric dips and curves. That's how massive objects like planets and stars warp spacetime around them. This isn't just some theoretical mumbo jumbo; it's how gravity works!

When you wrap your head around spacetime, you see how everything's linked. Your past, present, and future are all part of this grand tapestry. It's like a beautiful dance of cause and effect, where every little action sends ripples through the universe. This perspective packs a punch. It reminds us that our choices matter, that every moment is a thread in the intricate design of our lives.

Now, let's take a breather and reflect on what all this means. Time dilation and the idea of spacetime push us to rethink our existence. They remind us that life isn't just about the minutes ticking away on a clock. It's about experiences, relationships, and the bonds we build.

Think about it—when you're lost in a gripping book or having a heart-to-heart with a friend, time seems to fly by. That's the magic of spacetime doing its thing! It's a nudge to savor the moments, to be present in our lives. We're not just passive spectators; we're active players in this grand cosmic drama.

As we dig deeper into Einstein's Theory of Relativity, let's hold onto this understanding. Time isn't just a straight path; it's a rich tapestry of experiences waiting to be woven. Embrace the mystery, the wonder, and the beauty of spacetime. Your journey is just kicking off, and the universe has so much more to reveal.

Now, as we move on, remember this: every challenge is a chance to grow. Just like Einstein faced his share of skepticism and doubt, you too can navigate the twists and turns of your own journey. Trust in your potential, and let the principles of relativity inspire you to explore new frontiers. You got this!

Alright, let's keep rolling. What's next? Well, let's dig into general relativity. This is where things really get spicy. Einstein took his ideas about special relativity and expanded them to include gravity. Instead of thinking of gravity as some invisible force pulling things together, he showed it's all about the curvature of spacetime.

Think of it this way: imagine you're at a party, and you see a bunch of people standing around a trampoline. If someone heavy jumps on it, the trampoline sags, right? Now, if you roll a marble near that sag, it'll spiral inwards, drawn to the weight in the center. That's kinda how gravity works in Einstein's world. Massive objects like the Earth and the Sun create dips in spacetime, and other objects move along those curves. It's not just a force; it's the shape of spacetime guiding everything.

This idea blew minds back in the day. It meant that light itself could be affected by gravity. If a star's light passes near a massive object, it bends! This was proven during a solar eclipse in 1919 when scientists observed starlight curving around the Sun. Talk about a game-changer!

So, what does this mean for us? Well, it gives us a whole new way to look at the universe. We're not just floating in empty space; we're part of a dynamic, interconnected system. Every mass, every planet, every star is influencing the others. It's like a cosmic dance party, where everything's grooving together, and the beat is spacetime.

But wait, there's more! Let's chat about black holes. These bad boys are like the rock stars of general relativity. When a massive star collapses, it creates such a strong gravitational pull that not even light can escape. They're the ultimate spacetime traps. You get too close, and bam—you're gone! It's like being sucked into a cosmic vacuum cleaner.

Black holes challenge our understanding of physics. Inside, the rules we know break down. Time and space get all mixed up, and we're left with more questions than answers. It's a wild ride, and scientists are still trying to figure out what's going on in there.

And speaking of wild rides, let's talk about wormholes. These are hypothetical passages through spacetime that could create shortcuts between distant points in the universe. Imagine being able to hop from one galaxy to another in the blink of an eye! Sounds cool, right? But here's the catch: we haven't found any wormholes yet, and even if they exist, who knows if we could actually travel through them. It's all still in the realm of theory, but it's fun to think about!

Now, let's bring it back to Earth. What does all this mean for our daily lives? Well, it's a reminder that we're part of something way bigger than ourselves. Our actions, our choices, they ripple out into the universe. It's like tossing a pebble into a pond; the ripples spread out, affecting everything around them.

Think about your own life. Every time you lend a hand to someone, every time you share a laugh, you're weaving your own thread into the tapestry of spacetime. You're not just living in a vacuum; you're part of a vibrant, interconnected web of existence.

So, as we wrap this up, let's remember the essence of Einstein's Theory of Relativity. It's not just a set of equations or concepts; it's a way of seeing the world. Time and space are fluid, interconnected, and full of potential. They remind us to cherish our moments, to connect with others, and to embrace the mysteries of the universe.

And hey, don't forget to look up at the stars once in a while. They're a reminder of how small we are in the grand scheme of things, but also how beautiful it is to be part of this cosmic dance. Life's a journey, and every twist and turn is an opportunity to learn and grow. So, keep exploring, keep questioning, and most importantly, keep enjoying the ride. The universe is waiting for you!

Chapter 3

Gravity and Time

So, when you hear the word "gravity," what pops into your head? Maybe it's that classic story of the apple bonking Newton on the noggin or the gut-wrenching drop on a roller coaster. But here's the twist—gravity isn't just about keeping us glued to the ground. Nope, it's also got a hand in the whole time thing. Yup, gravity can actually bend time, and once you start to wrap your head around it, it's a wild ride.

Let's set the scene. You're standing on Earth, feeling the weight of your body. That heaviness? That's gravity at work. But hold up—what if I told you that the stronger the gravitational pull, the slower time moves? Sounds like something straight outta a sci-fi flick, right? But it's the real deal. This funky phenomenon is called gravitational time dilation. It's like gravity's hidden superpower, messing with how we experience time based on where we hang out in relation to big ol' massive objects.

Let's break it down. Picture yourself in a spaceship, just chilling near a black hole. Now, black holes are like the heavyweight champs of the universe. Their gravity? Off the charts. If you were to hover close to one, time for you would crawl by compared to someone just kicking back on Earth. It's as if the universe is saying, "Wanna take it slow? Just chill near that massive thing, and I'll stretch out time for ya." This ain't just some theoretical mumbo jumbo; scientists have backed it up with solid experimental evidence.

Take a look at the experiments with atomic clocks. These bad boys can measure time with insane precision. Researchers shot these clocks up into satellites, putting them in a weaker gravitational field than clocks chilling on Earth. And guess what? The clocks in space ticked just a smidge faster than those down on the ground. This isn't just a quirky detail; it's a crystal-clear example of how gravity messes with time. The higher you go, the less gravity you feel, and the faster time speeds up. It's like the universe has its own playbook, and we're just trying to keep up with the rules.

Now, let's chat about how massive objects shape our perception of time. Think about it: when you're near something huge—like a mountain or a towering skyscraper—you feel that rush of awe, right? You feel tiny. That feeling's got gravity written all over it. The bigger the object, the stronger its gravitational pull, and the more it can twist your experience of time. When you're surrounded by giants, time can feel like it's stretching out, making those moments feel longer and more meaningful. It's kinda like being in a dream where everything moves in slow-mo, and you can really soak in every second.

But wait, it gets even more interesting. In the wild world of quantum mechanics, the rules shift again. The tango between gravity and time is a complicated one, and we're just scratching the surface. The effects of gravitational time dilation ripple through our understanding of the universe, influencing everything from black holes to the very fabric of spacetime itself.

Let's think about this: if you were to zoom close to the speed of light while near a massive object, the combo of speed and gravity would create a time-warping experience like no other. You could blast off into the cosmos, and while you might age only a couple of years, decades could fly by for those back on Earth. Crazy, right? The universe is full of surprises, and gravity's a key player in this cosmic drama.

So, what's all this mean for you, the curious reader? It's a nudge to remember that time isn't just a straight line; it's more like a winding river, bending and twisting under gravity's influence. Next time you gaze up at the stars or feel the Earth's pull beneath your feet, take a sec to appreciate the intricate dance of gravity and time. It's a powerful reminder that our universe is a wonderland, packed with mysteries just waiting to be uncovered.

As you dive deeper into the science of time travel, keep in mind that every bump in the road you hit while trying to understand these concepts is just another chance to grow. You're taking a plunge into the deep end of knowledge, and that's where the real magic happens. Embrace the complexity, savor those "aha!" moments, and let your curiosity guide you. You've got this!

Now, let's explore some of the real-world implications of this mind-bending relationship between gravity and time. Have you ever heard of GPS? Yeah, those little satellites that help you navigate your way around town? Well, they're a perfect example of how gravitational time dilation plays out in our everyday lives. These satellites orbit Earth at a higher altitude, meaning they experience less gravitational pull than clocks on the ground,

Because of this, the clocks on the satellites tick faster than those on Earth. If scientists didn't account for this time difference, your GPS would be off by miles! It's wild to think that something as simple as getting directions relies on these cosmic principles.

Let's switch gears a bit and talk about black holes. They're like the rock stars of the universe— mysterious, powerful, and totally captivating. When we talk about black holes, we're diving into the deep end of gravity and time. You see, when something gets too close to a black hole, it experiences extreme gravitational forces. This can lead to some wild effects on time. Imagine a spaceship getting sucked into a black hole. For the crew on board, time would slow down dramatically as they approached the event horizon, the point of no return. Meanwhile, for observers far away, it would look like the spaceship was frozen in time. This raises some serious questions about what happens to time and space at such extremes.

And here's a thought—what if we could harness this knowledge? Imagine if we could create technology that allows us to manipulate time in some way. Time travel, anyone? Sure, it sounds like a plot twist from a blockbuster movie, but the science behind it isn't entirely far-fetched. Theoretical physicists have proposed ideas like wormholes—tunnels through spacetime that could connect distant points in the universe. While we're not quite there yet, it's a tantalizing idea that keeps scientists up at night.

Let's not forget about our own experiences with time. Ever notice how time seems to fly when you're having fun but drags when you're stuck in a boring meeting? That's a form of time dilation, too! Our perception of time can be influenced by our emotions and experiences. When you're engaged and enjoying yourself, time feels like it's speeding up. But during those dull moments, it stretches out like taffy. It's fascinating how our minds can play tricks on us, much like the universe does with gravity.

Now, let's throw in a little humor here. Have you ever thought about how gravity is like that friend who always keeps you grounded? You know, the one who's always there to remind you not to get too carried away? Gravity's that friend, keeping us in check, making sure we don't float off into the stratosphere. But just like that friend, gravity has its quirks. It's got its serious side, bending time and space, but it can also be a bit of a jokester, messing with our perceptions and experiences.

So, what's the takeaway from all this? The relationship between gravity and time is a wild ride, full of twists and turns. It's a reminder that our universe is a complex, interconnected web of phenomena. Gravity's not just a force; it's a player in the grand game of time. And as we continue to explore these concepts, we'll uncover more of the universe's secrets, one mind-bending revelation at a time.

As you journey through this cosmic landscape, remember to keep your sense of wonder alive. Don't shy away from the complexities; embrace them! Curiosity is your best ally, and every question you ask is a step closer to understanding the mysteries of existence. So, whether you're pondering the nature of time or simply enjoying a beautiful day on Earth, take a moment to appreciate the incredible interplay of gravity and time. It's a dance as old as the universe itself, and you're right in the middle of it.

In closing, let's not forget to look up at the night sky once in a while. The stars, the planets, the galaxies—they're all part of this grand cosmic story. And as you gaze into the vastness of space, remember that you're not just a spectator; you're part of this incredible journey. Gravity and time are your companions, guiding you through the wonders of the universe. So go ahead, embrace the mysteries, ask the tough questions, and let your curiosity lead the way. The universe is waiting for you to explore its secrets, one mind-boggling discovery at a time. You've got this!

Chapter 4

The Speed of Light

Light. It's not just that bright flash that blinds you when you step outside or the cozy glow of a lamp on a chilly night. Nah, it's way more than that. Light is the backbone of how we get a grip on this vast universe we live in. When we dive into the speed of light, we're really plunging into the deep end of physics, folks. Light zips along at roughly 299,792 kilometers per second. That's fast—like, if you blink, you'll miss it fast. This isn't just a random number; it's a fundamental constant of nature. Think of it as the cosmic speed limit, shaping the very fabric of reality. In physics, the speed of light is more than just a metric; it's a doorway to understanding how time and space tango together in this grand cosmic dance.

So, let's take a breather and think about what this speed means for us, especially when we start dreaming about time travel. Ever fantasized about zipping back to the past? Maybe to hang out with a younger version of yourself or catch a glimpse of some epic historical moment? Well, hold up! The speed of light kinda throws a wrench in those daydreams. Why? Because, according to Einstein's theory of relativity, nothing can outrun light. So, no matter how much we wish we could jump through time like some superhero, we're stuck with this cosmic rule. It's like trying to outrun your shadow—it just ain't happening.

Picture this: if you hopped on a spaceship and zoomed off at light speed, time would play tricks on you. This phenomenon? It's called time dilation. Imagine you're cruising through the cosmos, having the adventure of a lifetime, while back on Earth, time's just ticking away like usual. When you finally come back, you might find that years have flown by for everyone else, while you've only experienced a few moments. It's a wild concept, but it's a direct result of light speed being the ultimate speed limit.

But let's dig a little deeper. The connection between light and our sense of time is a rabbit hole worth exploring. Ever noticed how time seems to zip by when you're having a blast, yet drags on forever when you're bored out of your mind? That's not just some weird quirk of human nature; it's tied to how we process light. Our brains take in visual info based on the speed of light, and that messes with how we perceive time. In a way, light's like a metronome for our experiences. The faster it travels, the quicker we think things are happening. Slow it down, and suddenly, everything feels like it's crawling.

Now, let's take a step back and think about light's role in our everyday lives. Ever thought about how seeing works? When you flick on a lamp, that light zips to your eyes, letting you see the world around you. But that light does more than just brighten things up; it's also intertwined with time. Every second you spend in the light is shaped by how fast that light is moving. It's a beautiful reminder that time isn't just something we clock; it's something we live.

Let's not forget about the limits light speed puts on time travel. Imagine a time machine that could whisk you off to any moment in history. Sounds amazing, right? But here's the kicker: to jump through time like that, you'd need to mess with light speed—something we can't do just yet. You'd have to figure out how to bend the laws of physics, and that's no walk in the park. The universe has its own rules, and light speed is a cornerstone. It's like trying to break a world record; you can't just wish it into existence. You need training, strategy, and sometimes a sprinkle of luck.

As we wander through this intricate relationship between light and time, let's not overlook the wonders of quantum mechanics. This field opens up a whole new can of worms, including the mind-blowing idea of parallel universes. While we're still piecing together how time travel might actually work, the implications of light speed remind us that our universe is brimming with mysteries just waiting to be cracked open.

In a nutshell, the speed of light is like a beacon guiding us through the complexities of time. It teaches us about the limitations we face while also firing us up to push the boundaries of what we know. So, as you ponder the mysteries of time travel, keep this in mind: light isn't just a tool for seeing; it's a reminder of the intricate dance between time and space—a cosmic rhythm we're all part of.

Now, let's take a moment to think about how this knowledge can empower you. When you grasp the significance of light speed, you unlock a deeper understanding of your place in the universe. You're not just sitting on the sidelines; you're an active player in this grand cosmic story. So, embrace the wonder, keep questioning, and let the speed of light illuminate your path as you navigate the complexities of time and existence.

The journey of understanding light and its relationship with time is just the tip of the iceberg.

Each revelation you uncover adds another layer to your grasp of the universe. So, keep that curiosity burning bright, and let it lead you deeper into the fascinating world of time travel. The possibilities are endless, and the adventure is just getting warmed up.

Now, let's get real for a second. Ever had one of those days where you're just sitting around, and time feels like it's moving at a snail's pace? You know, when you're stuck in a boring meeting or waiting for your food at a restaurant? That's the kind of stuff that makes you realize how much we take light for granted. Think about it: without light, we'd be in total darkness, and our sense of time would be completely messed up.

When you flip that switch and light floods the room, it's not just about being able to see; it's about creating moments. Each second illuminated is a second lived. The speed of light connects us to everything around us. It's like the universe's way of keeping us in sync.

And speaking of synchronicity, have you ever thought about how light connects us across vast distances? Like, when you look up at the stars, the light you're seeing might have traveled for millions of years to reach your eyes. You're literally peeking into the past! That's some heavy stuff right there. It makes you feel small yet connected to something way bigger than yourself.

Let's chat about how this whole light-speed thing plays into our dreams of time travel. Imagine you could hop into a time machine and visit the dinosaurs. Cool, right? But to make that happen, you'd need to figure out how to bend time and space, and that's where light speed comes into play. You'd need to figure out how to manipulate the very fabric of the universe.

Now, here's where it gets a bit wild. Quantum mechanics suggests that time might not be as linear as we think. Some theories toss around the idea of multiple timelines or parallel universes. What if every choice you make creates a new timeline? It's mind-boggling, right? The implications of light speed and time travel could mean that every moment is a chance to explore a different path.

And let's not forget about the technological advances we're making. Scientists are always pushing the envelope, trying to find ways to harness the speed of light. From fiber optics to quantum computing, we're constantly finding new ways to use light to our advantage. Who knows? Maybe one day, we'll figure out how to travel through time, or at least find a way to manipulate our perception of it.

But here's a thought: what if we don't need a time machine to experience time travel? What if the real journey is about how we perceive our own lives? Time might feel like it's racing by when we're busy or having fun, but when we take a moment to slow down and appreciate the little things, it stretches out. It's like when you're on vacation—time feels different because you're fully present, soaking in every moment.

So, as you ponder the mysteries of light and time, don't just think about the big cosmic questions. Think about how this knowledge can enrich your everyday life. Embrace the moments that matter. Whether it's a sunset, a shared laugh, or a quiet moment of reflection, those are the times that make life worth living.

Now, let's wrap this up. The speed of light isn't just a scientific concept; it's a reminder of our place in the universe. It's about the connections we share, the moments we create, and the mysteries we still have to unravel. So, keep that curiosity alive, keep questioning, and let the wonders of light guide you through the beautiful chaos of existence.

And remember, the journey of understanding light and time is just beginning. Each step you take into this fascinating world adds another layer to your comprehension of the universe. So, keep exploring, keep dreaming, and who knows? Maybe one day, you'll find yourself on the brink of a time travel adventure of your own. The possibilities are endless, and the adventure? Well, it's just getting started.

Chapter 5

Quantum Mechanics Explained

When you think about the universe, it's easy to feel like a tiny speck lost in a vast, swirling cosmos. But hold onto your hat, because quantum mechanics is here to shake things up and turn your understanding of reality on its head. Imagine a world where particles can be in two places at once, where everything is connected in ways that defy common sense. That's the magic of quantum mechanics, and it's a game-changer when it comes to our understanding of time.

Let's kick things off with the foundational principles of quantum mechanics. At its core, this field of physics reveals that the universe operates on a level far different from what we experience in our day-to-day lives. Classical physics, with its neat and tidy rules, starts to crumble when you dive into the quantum realm. Here, uncertainty reigns supreme. You see, particles aren't just little marbles bouncing around; they exist in a state of probability. Instead of saying, "This particle is here," we say, "There's a chance it could be here, or here, or even over there." It's like trying to catch smoke with your bare hands—elusive and unpredictable.

Now, let's talk about superposition and entanglement—two concepts that will blow your mind and leave you questioning everything you thought you knew. Superposition is the idea that a particle can exist in multiple states at once until it's measured. Picture a spinning coin. As long as it's in the air, it's both heads and tails at the same time. It's only when you catch it that it lands on one side or the other. This principle opens the door to a universe where possibilities are endless, and outcomes aren't determined until we take a peek.

Then there's entanglement, which is like the universe's own version of a cosmic dance. When two particles become entangled, they're connected in such a way that the state of one instantly influences the state of the other, no matter how far apart they are. It's as if they're whispering secrets to each other across the cosmos. Imagine you and your best friend have a special bond—no matter the distance, you can feel what the other is feeling. That's entanglement in action, and it challenges our traditional notions of space and time.

Now, let's tie these concepts back to time, because that's where things get really interesting. In classical physics, time is linear, a straight path from past to present to future. But quantum mechanics throws a wrench in that neat little timeline. The implications of superposition and entanglement suggest that time may not be as straightforward as we think. If particles can exist in multiple states and be connected across vast distances, what does that mean for our understanding of time? Could it be that time itself is a more fluid concept, bending and warping in ways we can't yet comprehend?

Consider this: if you take a moment to reflect on your life, you might find that memories don't just flow in one direction. You may recall a childhood event that feels as vivid today as it did back then. Or perhaps you've had moments of déjà vu that make you feel like you've stepped back into a past experience. Quantum mechanics hints at the possibility that time might not be the rigid ruler we've always believed it to be. Instead, it could be a tapestry woven with threads of potentiality and connection, where the past, present, and future intertwine in ways we're just beginning to explore.

So, what does all this mean for you, the curious reader? It means that you have the power to shift your perspective. When you embrace the principles of quantum mechanics, you open yourself up to a world of possibilities. Just like particles that can exist in superposition, you too can explore multiple paths in your life. Don't let the fear of the unknown hold you back. Dive into new experiences, take risks, and see where they lead you.

Remember, the universe is vast, and your potential is even vaster. You're not just a passive observer; you're an active participant in the dance of existence. Just as entangled particles are interconnected, so too are you with the people and experiences around you. Every choice you make ripples through time, shaping not just your own life but the lives of others.

Now, let's break this down into some actionable steps.

First, embrace uncertainty. Life is full of surprises, and that's what makes it beautiful. When you face challenges, remind yourself that uncertainty is an opportunity for growth. Just like in quantum mechanics, where the act of observation changes the outcome, your perspective can change your reality.

Second, cultivate connections. Reach out to others, share your experiences, and build a network of support. You never know how your journey might inspire someone else or how their journey might impact you. Remember, you're all part of the same cosmic dance.

Finally, stay curious. Dive deeper into the world of quantum mechanics and its implications. Read books, watch documentaries, and engage in discussions. The more you learn, the more you'll realize that the universe is a playground of possibilities, waiting for you to explore.

As we wrap up this exploration of quantum mechanics, remember this: you are not just a spectator in the theater of life. You're a co-creator, a participant in the grand adventure of existence. Embrace the unknown, celebrate the connections, and let your curiosity guide you. The universe is yours to discover, and time is but a canvas for your imagination. So go out there, take a leap, and watch as the possibilities unfold before you.

Chapter 6

The Multiverse Theory

Picture this: a universe where every choice you've ever made branches off into its own reality. Sounds like something outta a sci-fi flick, right? But hang on a second—this is the multiverse theory, and it's a mind-bending concept that's got scientists buzzing like bees in spring. It suggests that our universe is just one of many, each with its own set of rules, realities, and timelines. Imagine standing at a crossroads, and every direction you could take creates a new universe. That's the multiverse in a nutshell—an infinite tapestry of possibilities woven together, each thread representing a different version of existence.

Now, let's dive into the nitty-gritty. There are several interpretations of the multiverse, and each one adds its own flavor to this cosmic stew. First up, we got the Many-Worlds Interpretation. This bad boy comes from quantum mechanics, suggesting that every time a quantum event happens—like flipping a coin—two outcomes occur simultaneously in separate universes. You could say it's like being at a family reunion where every relative shows up in their own unique outfit, all living their own lives in parallel.

Then there's the Bubble Universe theory, which posits that our universe is just one bubble in a frothy sea of bubbles, each representing a different universe. Picture a cosmic champagne party, where each bubble is a separate universe with its own laws of physics. Some might be similar to ours, while others could be so different they'd make your head spin.

And don't forget about the String Theory multiverse, where the fabric of reality is made up of tiny vibrating strings. This theory suggests there could be a whole bunch of dimensions we can't even perceive, leading to a universe teeming with potential realities. Each of these interpretations adds layers to our understanding of existence, like a delicious seven-layer dip at a potluck—each layer is distinct, yet they all come together to create something truly special.

Now, you might be wondering how all this ties into time travel. Well, hold onto your hats, because this is where things get really interesting. If the multiverse is real, then time travel could take on a whole new meaning. Instead of simply jumping back and forth within a single timeline, you could potentially leap into an alternate universe. Imagine traveling back to meet your younger self but instead of altering your past, you just create a new reality where things play out differently. It's like stepping into a different movie theater and watching a completely different film, even though it stars the same actors.

This idea opens up a treasure chest of possibilities. You could explore alternate histories, where pivotal moments in time went a different way. What if the dinosaurs never went extinct? Or what if you had chosen a different career path? Each choice creates a new universe, and with the right technology—or a good dose of imagination—you could navigate through these infinite timelines. It's like being a kid in a candy store, except instead of sweets, you're surrounded by an endless array of "what ifs."

But let's not get ahead of ourselves. There are still plenty of challenges to tackle when it comes to time travel and the multiverse. For one, the sheer complexity of navigating multiple realities is enough to make anyone's head spin. And then there's the question of causality—if you change something in one universe, what ripple effects does that have on others? It's a tangled web of consequences, and understanding it is like trying to solve a Rubik's cube blindfolded.

So, what does all this mean for you? Well, it means that the universe is far more complex and beautiful than we often realize. It's a reminder that every choice you make matters, not just in your life, but in the grand scheme of existence. Your decisions could be creating alternate realities, each one a testament to the paths not taken. Embrace that idea!

As you explore the multiverse theory, let it inspire you. Think about your own life as a series of branching paths. Each moment is a choice, a chance to create something new. And who knows? Maybe one day, with the right breakthroughs in science, we'll find a way to travel those paths. For now, though, let's savor the journey of understanding this incredible universe we inhabit.

In the end, the multiverse theory isn't just about physics and quantum mechanics; it's about the infinite potential of life itself. It's about dreaming big, believing in possibilities, and recognizing that your story is part of a much larger narrative. So, keep writing your own chapters, exploring your own universes, and remember: the journey is just as important as the destination. You got this!

Chapter 7

Time Travel in Fiction vs. Reality

When you hear "time travel," what comes to mind? Maybe you picture that iconic DeLorean flying through a time vortex, or perhaps you think of those wild twists in a sci-fi novel that make you question reality. Time travel has been a hot topic for ages, popping up in books, movies, and even our casual chats. But what's the real deal with this mind-bending concept? Let's take a deep dive into the fascinating world of time travel stories, the science behind it, and how these tales impact our culture.

Let's kick things off by wandering through some popular time travel stories. Think of H.G. Wells' "The Time Machine" or the zany adventures in "Doctor

Who." These narratives have colored our perception of what time travel could be. They paint these vivid scenes of jumping through time, shaking hands with historical figures, or peeking into the future. Characters like Marty McFly remind us that our past choices can either bite us in the butt or save our skins. These aren't just fun tales; they make us ponder our own timelines and the decisions we make.

But here's where it gets juicy. While these stories spark our imaginations, the science of time travel is a whole different kettle of fish. Scientists have been scratching their heads over whether time travel could actually happen. Einstein's theory of relativity cracks the door open a bit, introducing concepts like time dilation, where time ticks differently based on speed and gravity. But let's be honest—jumping into a time machine and zooming back to the past? Yeah, that's still a fantasy.

Still, there's a flicker of hope in the scientific world. Theoretical ideas like wormholes and the multiverse theory suggest that time travel might not be a total pipe dream. Wormholes could serve as shortcuts through spacetime, while the multiverse theory hints that every choice we make spawns a new timeline. It's a wild ride, and while we're not booking our tickets for a time-travel adventure just yet, it's thrilling to think about what could be.

Now, let's hit the brakes and think about how these time travel stories affect us culturally. They hit home, don't they? At their core, these narratives tackle themes like regret, nostalgia, and the longing to rewrite our destinies. They remind us that time is a precious commodity. We all have moments we wish we could revisit or change. Engaging with these tales isn't just about entertainment; it's a chance to reflect on our lives, our connections, and the choices that define us.

Take "Back to the Future," for instance. It's not just about the thrill of time travel; it dives into family, friendship, and the need to seize the moment. These stories push us to look back at our past and think about how we can steer our futures. They remind us that while we can't rewrite history, we have the power to mold what's ahead.

And let's not overlook the discussions these stories kick off. They challenge how we see time, reality, and existence. They get us thinking about the implications of time travel—what it means for causality, free will, and our grasp of the universe. They create a shared lingo among us, connecting folks across generations and cultures as we ponder the great unknown together.

So, what's the takeaway from this chat about time travel in fiction versus reality? For starters, let's appreciate the magic of storytelling. These narratives let us dream, question, and reflect. They remind us that while the science of time travel might still be in its infancy, our urge to explore and understand is as timeless as time itself.

Now, embrace that curiosity! Whether you're a writer or a reader, let these stories fuel your imagination. Dive into the realm of time travel, and let your creativity run wild. Who knows? You might stumble upon a gem of wisdom that resonates with your own journey. And as you do, remember that every story, every choice, and every moment is a step in the dance of time. So go ahead, take that leap of faith, and see where your timeline takes you. Adventure awaits!

Alright, let's dig a little deeper. Why do we love time travel stories so much? Maybe it's the thrill of the unknown. The idea of bending the rules of time and space is tantalizing. We've all had those "what if" moments—what if I could go back and tell my younger self to study harder, or what if I could see what the future holds? Time travel stories let us explore those "what ifs" in a safe space.

Think about it: time travel gives us a chance to relive our best moments or fix our biggest mistakes. Ever wished you could go back and change a breakup or a job decision? That's the allure of time travel. It's not just about the mechanics of jumping through time;

it's about the emotional journey that comes with it. It's a way to confront our regrets and dream about second chances.

And let's not forget the sheer creativity involved in these stories. Writers have a blast crafting complex plots that weave through different timelines. Some stories stick to the classic rules—if you change something in the past, it messes up the future. Others throw those rules out the window, leading to all sorts of wild scenarios. It's like a playground for the imagination.

Then there's the moral aspect. Time travel stories often come with ethical dilemmas. If you could change history, should you? What if your actions in the past have unforeseen consequences? These questions make us think critically about our own lives and the impact of our choices. It's a fascinating way to explore the human experience.

And speaking of exploration, let's chat about the different ways time travel is portrayed across cultures. In some cultures, time is viewed as cyclical, while in others, it's linear. This perspective shapes how time travel stories are told. For instance, in many Western narratives, time travel often revolves around the individual's journey—how one person's choices can change everything. In contrast, some Eastern philosophies emphasize collective experiences and interconnectedness, leading to narratives that focus on community and shared destinies.

Think about movies like "Groundhog Day." It's not just about reliving the same day over and over; it's about personal growth and the impact of one's actions on others. The protagonist learns that his choices affect the people around him, which ties into that collective experience idea. It's a reminder that we're all part of a bigger picture, even when we're navigating our own timelines.

Now, let's talk about the science behind all this. Sure, it sounds like a wild fantasy, but there are real scientists out there exploring these concepts. Take wormholes, for example. They're hypothetical passages through spacetime that could connect distant points in time and space. It's like a cosmic shortcut! If they exist, they could potentially allow for time travel. But here's the kicker—nobody's actually found one yet. It's all theoretical, but it's fun to think about.

And what about black holes? They're another fascinating piece of the puzzle. Some theories suggest that if you could survive the intense gravity of a black hole, you might be able to emerge in a different time or place. Again, it's all speculation, but the science behind it is mind-blowing. It shows how the universe is filled with mysteries waiting to be unraveled.

But let's not get too lost in the science. The real magic of time travel stories lies in their ability to resonate with us emotionally. They tap into our deepest fears and desires. We all want to feel in control of our destinies, and these narratives offer a glimpse of that power. They remind us that while we can't change the past, we can learn from it and make choices that shape our futures.

And here's a thought: time travel isn't just about the past or future; it's also about the present. Every moment we live is a step in our personal timeline. The choices we make today impact who we become tomorrow. Time travel stories remind us to cherish the present, to seize the moment, and to make the most of our time.

So, what's next? Let's talk about how you can engage with these ideas. Whether you're a fan of reading, writing, or just daydreaming, there's a whole world of time travel to explore. Pick up a classic like "The Time Machine" or binge-watch "Doctor Who." You might even want to try your hand at writing your own time travel story. Who knows where your imagination might take you?

And remember, the beauty of time travel is that it's not just about escaping reality; it's about confronting it. It's about reflecting on who we are and who we want to be. So, as you dive into these narratives, think about the lessons they offer. What can you learn from the characters' journeys? How can their experiences inspire your own?

In the end, time travel is more than just a sci-fi trope. It's a way for us to explore the human experience, to confront our regrets, and to dream about our futures. It's a testament to our desire to understand the world around us and our place in it. So go ahead, indulge in those time travel tales. Let them spark your imagination and inspire you to think about your own journey through time. The adventure is just beginning!

Chapter 8

The Grandfather Paradox

Imagine you've got a time machine, right? You hop in, twist a few knobs, and suddenly you're back in the past. Maybe you're at your grandfather's house, watching him as a young man. Now, here's where it gets sticky. What if you accidentally bump into him, or worse, you stop him from meeting your grandmother? Well, if that happens, you might never be born. So, if you were never born, how on Earth did you just travel back in time to mess with your grandpa in the first place? This, my friend, is the classic time travel paradox known as the Grandfather Paradox. It's a real head-scratcher, and it's got folks scratching their heads for decades.

The implications of this paradox reach deep into the heart of causality and free will. You see, causality is the idea that every effect has a cause. If you change the past, you mess with that chain of events. It raises a million questions: Do we have free will? If you could change the past, would you? And if you did, would you still have the same future? This paradox makes us wonder if time is a straight line or a tangled web.

Now, let's take a moment to unpack this. Causality, in simple terms, is like a row of dominoes. You tip the first one, and they all fall in a neat line. But what happens if you go back and tip a domino that you weren't supposed to? You've just created a mess, and that mess is the Grandfather Paradox. It shakes the very foundation of how we understand our choices and the paths we take in life. If we can change the past, do our choices even matter? Are we just puppets dancing to the strings of time?

But hold on! Before we spiral too deep into the rabbit hole, let's talk about some possible resolutions to this paradox. It's not all doom and gloom. There are theories out there that try to make sense of this conundrum. One popular idea is the concept of branching timelines. Picture this: when you travel back and change something, you don't alter your original timeline. Instead, you create a new branch. So, in one universe, you were born, and in another, you weren't. It's like flipping through a book and finding alternate endings.

Another resolution is the idea of self-consistency. This theory suggests that any actions you take in the past were always part of the timeline. In other words, you can't change the past because whatever you do was always meant to happen. It's like a cosmic game of "what's meant to be will be." This way, you can still visit your grandfather without worrying about your own existence being wiped out.

Now, let's not forget about the multiverse theory, which we've touched on before. In this view, every decision creates a new universe. So, if you went back and changed something, you'd just be hopping into a different universe altogether. Your original self still exists in the timeline where you were born, and the new you is off living in a universe where you didn't exist. It's a wild ride, but it sure makes for some fascinating possibilities!

So, what does all this mean for you? Well, the Grandfather Paradox isn't just a puzzle for physicists and philosophers. It's a reflection of our own lives and choices. We all have moments we wish we could change, paths we wish we could reroute. But the truth is, every decision we make shapes who we are. Even the mistakes, the wrong turns, and the bumps in the road—they all contribute to our unique journey.

As you sit with these ideas, I want you to think about your own life. What moments have shaped you? What choices have led you to where you are now? Just like the Grandfather Paradox, life is full of twists and turns, and it's our experiences that create the rich tapestry of who we are. Embrace those moments, and remember that every step, even the missteps, is part of your story.

In closing, the Grandfather Paradox invites us to ponder the nature of time, causality, and our own free will. It challenges us to think about the implications of our actions, not just in the context of time travel, but in our everyday lives. So, as you continue on this journey of understanding time and its mysteries, keep in mind that you have the power to shape your own narrative. Your choices matter, and they lead you to the beautiful, unpredictable journey that is your life.

Now, go ahead and take a moment to reflect. Picture your own timeline—what does it look like? What paths have you taken, and where do you want to go next? The future is yours to shape, and just like in the world of time travel, the possibilities are endless. Keep that spirit of curiosity alive, and remember, every twist and turn is an opportunity for growth and discovery. You got this!

Chapter 9

Wormholes and Time Travel

Imagine, if you will, a tunnel—a shortcut through the very fabric of space and time. That's the essence of a wormhole. It's a theoretical construct that stretches our imagination and tickles our intellect. Picture it as a bridge connecting two distant points in the universe. But hold on, it's not just about distance; it's about time, too. Wormholes could very well be the key to unlocking the secrets of time travel.

Now, let's break this down. A wormhole is like a cosmic cheat code. You see, in the realm of physics, we've got these mind-bending ideas that challenge our everyday experiences. Think of it as bending a piece of paper and poking a hole through it. You could travel from one side to the other without having to traverse the entire length. That's the beauty of a wormhole. It's a shortcut through spacetime, and if we could harness it, we might just be able to jump through time itself.

But here's where it gets tricky. The idea of using wormholes for time travel is as tantalizing as it is complex. Theoretically, if you could enter one end of a wormhole, you might pop out at a different point in time. Imagine stepping into a wormhole today and emerging in the past or future. Sounds like something straight outta a sci-fi flick, right? But we're talking about real physics here, folks! The potential is staggering, but so are the challenges.

Creating and sustaining a wormhole isn't exactly a walk in the park. We're not just talking about building a tunnel; we're diving into the deep end of theoretical physics. For starters, we'd need an immense amount of energy—think of it as powering a small star. We're talking about exotic matter, something that defies our current understanding of physics. This matter would need to have negative energy density, which is a concept that's hard to wrap your head around.

And then there's the stability issue. A wormhole could collapse in an instant, leaving anyone inside as toast. So, we'd have to figure out how to keep it open long enough for a person or a spaceship to make it through. It's like trying to hold a bubble underwater while also making sure it doesn't pop. The odds are stacked against us, but isn't that what makes this journey so thrilling?

Now, let's pause for a moment. Think about all the stories we've heard about time travel. The "what ifs" and "if onlys" that swirl around our minds. Wormholes offer a glimpse into that tantalizing possibility. They remind us that the universe is full of mysteries just waiting to be uncovered.

So, how do we tackle these challenges? First, we need to keep our minds open. Science is all about exploration, and the road to discovery is paved with curiosity and perseverance. Start by digging into the theoretical frameworks that surround wormholes. Read up on Einstein's theories and quantum mechanics. They're like the breadcrumbs leading you down a path of wonder.

Next, engage with the scientific community. Attend lectures, join discussions, and connect with those who share your passion for the cosmos. You'll find that the excitement is contagious. The more you learn, the more you'll see that the challenges of creating and sustaining wormholes aren't insurmountable; they're just stepping stones on the path to understanding.

Let's not forget the importance of collaboration. The greatest breakthroughs often come from diverse minds coming together. So, if you've got an idea, don't keep it to yourself. Share it! You never know who might take that spark and turn it into a blazing fire of innovation.

And remember, the journey of exploring wormholes and time travel isn't just about the destination; it's about the joy of discovery. Embrace the challenges as opportunities to grow and learn. Each question you ask, each theory you explore, brings you one step closer to understanding the universe and your place in it.

Now, I know it can feel overwhelming at times. But let me tell you, every great scientist faced hurdles. They stumbled, they fell, but they always got back up. That's the spirit you need to embody. Approach these challenges with a can-do attitude. If we can dream it, we can find a way to make it happen.

So, what's next? Start small. Take a moment to visualize what time travel could mean for you. Picture yourself stepping into a wormhole, feeling the rush of time bending around you. What would you do? Where would you go? Let that vision fuel your passion.

In conclusion, the world of wormholes and time travel is a vast, uncharted territory. It's a place where the impossible becomes possible, and the ordinary transforms into the extraordinary. So, dive in with enthusiasm! Embrace the challenges, harness your curiosity, and keep pushing the boundaries of what we know.

You've got this! The universe is waiting for you to explore its secrets, and who knows? Maybe one day, you'll be the one to unlock the mysteries of time travel for all of us. So, roll up your sleeves, open your mind, and let's journey into the unknown together!

Chapter 10

Temporal Mechanics

Alright, let's take a stroll through the mind-bending world of time travel, shall we? Buckle up, 'cause we're diving into some pretty wild concepts that twist reality like a pretzel. When we talk about time travel, we're not just chatting about hopping in a DeLorean or some sci-fi contraption. Nah, we're stepping into a universe where time isn't just a straight line; it's more like a tangled ball of yarn.

So, what's the deal with the theories behind time travel? Think of them as the framework holding up this crazy idea. They're like the skeleton of a massive building, giving structure to all those wild dreams we have about bending time. You know, those dreams where you wish you could go back and fix that one embarrassing moment from high school? Yeah, those dreams.

Let's get into the nitty-gritty. Theoretical frameworks are basically the science and math trying to explain how time travel might actually work. Sure, Einstein's theory of relativity is the big name in the game, but it's just scratching the surface. Dive deeper, and you hit quantum mechanics and multiverse theories. Each of these ideas is like a puzzle piece that, when put together, creates a picture of what time travel could be.

Now, here's where it gets really interesting: time loops. Imagine this scenario: you step into a time machine, and instead of just visiting the past, you find yourself stuck in a loop, reliving the same moment over and over. Sounds like a plot twist straight outta a Hollywood flick, right? But time loops aren't just for the big screen; they have some serious implications in the theoretical realm of time travel.

Let's think about it. If you're trapped in a time loop, what does that mean for your choices? Your actions? It's like being stuck in a video game where you can't get past a certain level. Are you really making decisions, or are you just following a script? It's a wild concept that flips our understanding of free will on its head. If you keep hitting the replay button, can you ever make a different choice? Or are you just a marionette, dancing to the tune of fate?

Now, let's toss entropy into the mix. Entropy is just a fancy word for disorder. Think of it like this: your room starts off clean, but the longer you ignore it, the messier it gets. That's entropy at work. In the context of time travel, entropy plays a crucial role. As time goes on, the universe tends to get messier. So, if you decide to hop back in time, can you really reverse that mess? Or are you just adding more chaos to an already chaotic system?

Here's the kicker: the second law of thermodynamics tells us that in a closed system, entropy can only increase. So, if you think you can jump back to fix a mistake, you might just end up creating a whole new mess. Time travel isn't all fun and games; it's like dancing with the laws of physics, and trust me, it can lead to some chaotic outcomes.

Let's take a step back and see how all these ideas connect. The theoretical frameworks, the implications of time loops, and the role of entropy all weave together like threads in a tapestry. They create a rich narrative that lets us explore the possibilities of time travel while keeping us grounded in the reality of the universe we live in.

As you mull over these concepts, don't forget that the magic of time travel isn't just in the mechanics. It's in the stories we tell and the questions we ponder. What if we could revisit our past and change a decision? What if we could take a sneak peek into the future? The possibilities are endless, but so are the challenges.

So, as you embark on this journey through the temporal mechanics of time travel, keep your mind wide open. Embrace the uncertainty and the wonder that comes with exploring the unknown. Every twist and turn in this adventure is a chance to learn, grow, and expand your understanding of what it means to exist in time.

Now, let's get a little personal. Picture this: you're at a family gathering, and someone brings up that one time you spilled grape juice all over your aunt's new carpet. You cringe, wishing you could rewind and do it all over again. Time travel, in this case, would be a lifesaver. But then you think—what if you went back and fixed that moment, only to mess up something else? Maybe you wouldn't have met your best friend later because of that one change. It's a slippery slope, isn't it?

And speaking of slopes, let's chat about the multiverse. The idea that every choice creates a new branch in the universe is mind-blowing. So, when you fix that grape juice incident, a new universe opens up where you're the hero who never spills. But in another universe, you're the klutz who spills again. It's like a cosmic game of "what if." Every decision creates a ripple effect, branching out into infinite possibilities.

Now, let's get a bit philosophical. What does it mean to exist in time? Are we just passengers on a train, watching the scenery change as we move forward? Or are we more like the conductor, able to pull the brakes and choose our stops? The concept of time is slippery, and trying to pin it down is like trying to catch smoke with your bare hands.

And let's not forget about causality—the relationship between cause and effect. If you go back and change something, what happens to the future? It's like throwing a rock into a pond; the ripples spread out, affecting everything around them. You could save a life, or you could accidentally cause a catastrophe. It's a heavy burden to bear, thinking about the consequences of our actions across time.

But hey, it's not all doom and gloom. Time travel opens up a world of creativity. Think about the stories we can tell! From H.G. Wells' "The Time Machine" to movies like "Interstellar," time travel gives us a canvas to explore human experiences, regrets, and dreams. It's a way to confront our past while imagining a future that could be different.

Let's take a quick detour to pop culture. Ever seen "Groundhog Day"? It's a classic example of a time loop. Bill Murray's character, Phil, is stuck reliving the same day until he learns some valuable life lessons. It's funny, poignant, and a perfect illustration of how time loops can challenge our understanding of growth and change. If you're stuck in a loop, how do you break free? What lessons do you need to learn?

Now, let's bring it back to reality. While time travel may seem like a far-off fantasy, scientists are actually dabbling in some pretty cool stuff. Take wormholes, for instance. They're theoretical passages through space-time that could create shortcuts for long journeys across the universe. It's like finding a secret tunnel that leads you to your destination faster. But here's the catch: we're still figuring out how to create or stabilize these wormholes. It's all theoretical, but it gives us hope that maybe, just maybe, time travel isn't as far-fetched as it seems.

And speaking of hope, let's talk about the human experience. We're all grappling with the passage of time. Aging, memories, regrets—these are all part of our journey. Time travel, in a way, lets us confront these issues. What would you change if you could? Would you take back that hurtful thing you said? Would you savor those fleeting moments with loved ones?

In the end, time travel isn't just about the mechanics; it's about us—our choices, our regrets, our dreams. It invites us to engage with the universe in a profound way. It's a reminder that time isn't just a straight line; it's a vast, intricate web of possibilities.

So, grab your metaphorical time machine and let's explore this wondrous world of temporal mechanics. Embrace the uncertainty, the chaos, and the beauty of it all. Because whether you're a dreamer, a scientist, or just a curious soul, the exploration of time travel is an adventure worth taking. It's a journey that challenges us to think deeply about our existence and the choices we make along the way.

And who knows? Maybe one day, we'll crack the code and find a way to travel through time. Until then, let's keep dreaming, questioning, and exploring the infinite possibilities that lie ahead. After all, the future is unwritten, and the past is just a memory. So, let's make the most of the time we have and see where this wild ride takes us!

Chapter 11

Philosophical Implications of Time Travel

Time travel ain't just about zipping back to the past or leaping into the future. No sir, it digs deep into the roots of our existence, raising questions that tickle the mind and tug at the heart. When we think about the nature of reality and existence, we gotta wonder: what's real? What's just a figment of our imagination? If we can hop through time, does that mean reality is more fluid than we ever thought? Picture this: every moment we live creates ripples in the fabric of existence. Every choice, every action, they shape not just our lives but the very essence of reality itself.

Now, let's talk about altering the past. That's where things get sticky. Imagine you could change a mistake—maybe you didn't say "I love you" when you had the chance, or you took a wrong turn in life that led you down a tough road. The temptation to go back and fix it is strong, right? But hold your horses! Every action has consequences, and the ethical considerations of time travel are a wild ride. If you change one little thing, what happens to the rest? It's like tossing a pebble into a pond—the ripples can go on forever, altering the course of countless lives.

So, let's break this down. If you decide to save someone from a tragic fate, what about the lives that might be affected by that choice? You could save one person but doom another. It's a moral conundrum, and it's enough to make your head spin. We gotta think about the bigger picture. Are we ready to bear the weight of those choices? Time travel could give us the power to reshape our destinies, but with great power comes great responsibility.

And what about personal identity? That's another kettle of fish. If you travel back in time and change your past, are you still the same person? It's a question that can make your brain ache. You see, our identities are woven from our experiences, memories, and choices. If you alter those threads, what happens to the tapestry of who you are? You might come back from your time jaunt as a completely different version of yourself. Maybe you're happier, maybe you're sadder, or maybe you're just... different.

Let's get real here. Time travel could lead to some serious identity crises. Imagine meeting your past self. What would you say? Would you recognize each other? Would you feel a connection, or would you be like two strangers passing in the night? It's a fascinating thought. Our past shapes us, but if we change it, we're stepping into uncharted waters.

In this grand adventure of time travel, we're not just playing with clocks and calendars. We're delving into the very essence of what it means to be human. The nature of reality, the ethics of our choices, and the fluidity of personal identity—all these threads are intricately woven together in the tapestry of time.

Now, let's dig a little deeper. The nature of reality is a slippery slope. We think we understand it, but what if it's all just a perception? What if reality shifts based on our experiences? Think about it: every time you remember something, you're not just recalling a moment; you're recreating it. You're adding layers, changing the context, and reshaping it into something new. Time travel could take this to a whole new level.

If we can visit different points in time, we might find that reality is a mosaic of experiences, a collection of moments that can be rearranged. What if we discover that there are multiple realities existing simultaneously? It's a wild idea, but it's one that resonates with the multiverse theory. Each choice we make could create a new branch of reality, leading to infinite possibilities.

This brings us to the ethical implications. If we can change our past, should we? It's a question that demands reflection. We're not just talking about personal choices; we're talking about the impact on others. Every time we alter a moment, we're playing God in a way. And that's a heavy burden to carry.

Consider the butterfly effect. A small change can lead to monumental shifts in the world. You save one life, but what about the lives that are intertwined with that fate? It's a ripple effect that could spiral out of control. We need to tread carefully, my friends. The power of time travel comes with the responsibility to consider the broader implications of our actions.

And let's not forget about personal identity. If we mess with our past, we might lose a piece of ourselves in the process. Our experiences shape who we are. They give us our stories, our wisdom, our scars. What happens if we take those away? We might find ourselves in a strange place, grappling with an identity that feels foreign.

Think about this: if you could go back and change a painful memory, would you? It's tempting, isn't it? But what if that pain taught you something valuable? What if it made you stronger? Our struggles are part of our journey, and they contribute to the richness of our lives.

So, as we ponder the philosophical implications of time travel, let's remember that it's not just about the mechanics of hopping through time. It's about understanding the weight of our choices, the fluidity of reality, and the essence of who we are.

Take a moment to reflect on your own life. Think about the choices you've made, the paths you've taken. Every decision has shaped you, molded you into the person you are today. If you could change one thing, would you? What would it mean for your identity?

As we navigate this journey, let's embrace the complexity of time travel. Let's explore the possibilities while staying grounded in our values. The adventure is thrilling, but it's also a chance for growth and understanding.

In the end, the philosophical implications of time travel remind us that we are not just travelers through time; we are stewards of our own destinies. Our choices matter, and the impact we have on ourselves and others is profound.

So, as you write your own story—whether it's a tale of time travel or a reflection on your life— remember to honor the journey. Embrace the lessons, cherish the moments, and don't shy away from the tough questions. Your voice, your perspective, and your experiences are what make your story unique.

Keep writing, keep exploring, and let the adventure unfold. You've got this!

Chapter 12

Technological Advances in Time Exploration

Alright, folks, let's dive into the wild world of time exploration. Picture this: you're stepping into a cosmic dance party where the universe throws its best mysteries at you. Trying to wrap your head around time? It's like chasing shadows—sometimes it slips right through your fingers, but man, is it exhilarating! Today, we're gonna unpack the latest scientific experiments pushing the limits of time, peek into what the future might hold for time travel tech, and see how AI is shaking things up. So strap in; it's gonna be a bumpy ride!

Let's start with the here and now. Scientists are cooking up some seriously mind-blowing experiments that challenge everything we think we know about time. Take CERN, for example. Researchers there are smashing particles together at speeds that make your head spin—literally! They're not just looking for flashy explosions; they're digging deep into the very fabric of spacetime. By studying what happens when these particles collide, they're gathering clues about the elusive nature of time. They're checking out how particles behave differently at various speeds and how that ties into time dilation—yep, the same thing Einstein was raving about ages ago.

But wait, it gets even cooler. We've got atomic clocks that are so precise they can measure time differences smaller than a blink over massive distances. These bad boys have been sent up in jets and even launched into space. And guess what? Time doesn't tick the same everywhere! It's like a cosmic game of tag, with time being the unpredictable player. These experiments not only back up Einstein's theories but also lay the groundwork for future tech that might let us mess with time itself.

Now, let's take a wild leap into the future. Time travel has always been a sci-fi dream, but with tech moving at lightning speed, it's starting to feel less like a fantasy and more like something we could actually do. Imagine if we could create stable wormholes—those theoretical shortcuts through spacetime. Scientists are brainstorming ways to generate and stabilize these portals, which could let us jump through time and space. We're not quite there yet, but hey, every great invention starts with a wild idea!

And speaking of wild ideas, let's talk about quantum computing. This tech is another frontier that could flip our understanding of time on its head. With its insane processing power, quantum computers might one day help us crack the complex equations that govern time travel. Think of it as having a supercharged calculator that can spit out answers on time travel theories in the blink of an eye. We're talking breakthroughs that could blow our minds!

And don't even get me started on artificial intelligence. Seriously, AI is shaking things up in every field, and time research is no exception. With its knack for analyzing massive amounts of data and spotting patterns faster than any human can, AI is becoming a key player in our quest to figure out time. Researchers are using machine learning algorithms to sift through experimental data, hunt down anomalies, and even suggest new theories. Imagine having an AI buddy that can simulate different time travel scenarios, helping us visualize what might happen before we even take the plunge. It's like having a crystal ball, but way more scientific!

Now, here's where it gets super exciting. The way AI integrates into time research isn't just about crunching numbers; it's about teamwork. Scientists are leveraging AI to boost their experiments, design better tools, and even predict the outcomes of time-related phenomena. This mix of human creativity and machine efficiency could turbocharge our understanding of time in ways we can't even wrap our heads around yet.

But let's not get too carried away. While the future looks bright, we've gotta keep our feet on the ground. There are challenges ahead. Creating tech that could enable time travel isn't just about overcoming scientific obstacles; it also raises some serious ethical questions. If we ever figure out how to time travel, what does that mean for causality? For the choices we make? These are heavy questions we'll need to wrestle with as we move forward.

As we wrap up this wild ride through the technological advances in time research, let's take a moment to appreciate the journey we're on. We're standing on the edge of discovery, with each experiment and tech leap inching us closer to unraveling the mysteries of time. It's a thrilling adventure, filled with potential and promise.

Remember, every small step in research is a giant leap for our understanding of the universe. You might not be in a lab, mixing chemicals or smashing particles, but you're part of this journey. Your curiosity, your questions, and your imagination are what fuel this exploration. So keep asking, keep dreaming, and who knows? One day, you might just find yourself on the brink of time travel, ready to hop into the past or leap into the future.

Now, let's keep our eyes on the stars and our minds open to the possibilities. The adventure has just begun!

Now, let's dig a little deeper into what's really happening in the world of time research. Scientists aren't just sitting around waiting for a miracle to happen. They're out there in the trenches, pushing the envelope and challenging the status quo. You've got teams at places like MIT and Stanford, where they're experimenting with everything from particle physics to cosmology. These folks are working hard to figure out the fundamental nature of time, and trust me, it's not as straightforward as it sounds.

One of the coolest experiments I've come across involves something called "time crystals." Now, don't let the name fool you. These aren't your grandma's crystals you'd find in a dusty old box. Time crystals are a state of matter that could theoretically exist in a way that defies the usual laws of physics. They oscillate in time, without consuming energy. It's like they're dancing through time, and researchers are scratching their heads trying to understand how this works. If they can unlock the secrets of time crystals, who knows what kind of tech we could develop?

Let's also talk about gravitational waves. Yeah, those ripples in spacetime that Einstein predicted over a century ago. They've been detected, and researchers are using them to study cosmic events. When two black holes collide, they send out gravitational waves that can tell us a lot about the nature of time and space. It's like eavesdropping on the universe's biggest secrets. This research could lead to breakthroughs that change our understanding of time itself.

And speaking of black holes, they're another fascinating area of study. These cosmic beasts warp spacetime around them, and studying them can give us insights into how time behaves under extreme conditions. It's like looking at time through a funhouse mirror—everything gets distorted. Scientists are using powerful telescopes and simulations to study these phenomena, and the findings could have implications for our understanding of time travel. Imagine being able to harness the power of a black hole!

But let's not forget about the philosophical side of things. Time isn't just a scientific concept; it's something we experience every day. It shapes our lives, our decisions, and our understanding of the universe. As we explore the technological advances in time research, we also need to consider the implications of what we're learning. If we ever figure out how to travel through time, how will that affect our relationships, our history, and our future? These are questions that need to be addressed as we venture into the unknown.

Now, let's circle back to AI. It's not just about analyzing data; it's about enhancing human capabilities. Imagine scientists using AI to design experiments that we can't even think of right now. With AI's ability to process information at lightning speed, it could help us uncover patterns in time research that we'd never see on our own. This partnership between humans and machines could lead to breakthroughs that change everything we know about time.

And what about the role of public engagement in all this? As researchers make strides in understanding time, it's crucial to bring the public along for the ride. Science isn't just for the lab coats and whiteboards; it's for everyone. We need to spark curiosity and ignite imaginations. Imagine a world where people are actively engaged in discussions about time travel, ethics, and the implications of new discoveries. That's the kind of future we should be aiming for.

So, as we stand on the brink of these incredible advancements, let's keep pushing the boundaries of what we know. Let's keep asking the tough questions and exploring the unknown. The journey into the mysteries of time is just beginning, and every one of us has a part to play.

In the end, it's about curiosity. It's about dreaming big and not being afraid to ask, "What if?" What if we could travel through time? What if we could manipulate spacetime? What if we could unlock the secrets of the universe? Those questions are what drive us forward. So let's keep our minds open, our spirits high, and our eyes on the stars. The adventure is just getting started, and who knows what we'll discover next?

As we wrap this up, remember that time exploration is a journey. It's not just about the destination; it's about the thrill of the chase, the excitement of discovery, and the joy of learning. So let's embrace the unknown, challenge the status quo, and keep pushing the limits of what's possible. The universe is out there, waiting for us to uncover its secrets. Let's get to it!

Chapter 13

Time Travel and Consciousness

Time and consciousness, well, they're two of the most fascinating puzzles we can dive into, don't ya think? They're like two dance partners swirling around in the grand ballroom of existence. One can't really move without the other, and understanding how they relate can unlock some pretty profound insights into our lives. So, let's take a stroll down this mind-bending path together.

First off, let's chew on the relationship between consciousness and time. You see, consciousness isn't just a passive observer; it's a dynamic player in how we experience time. Think of it like this: when you're fully present, time seems to stretch and expand. You know those moments when you're lost in a great conversation or immersed in a gripping book? Time flies, or maybe it stands still. That's your consciousness bending the fabric of time, shaping your perception of it. On the flip side, when you're anxious or bored, time drags on like molasses in January. Your mind can make time feel heavy, like a weight pressing down on your shoulders.

Now, let's dig a little deeper into altered states of consciousness. These states can really shake things up, offering a different lens through which to view time. Have you ever tried meditation or maybe taken a moment to just breathe? In those still, quiet moments, many folks report a feeling of timelessness. It's as if the clock has taken a vacation, and you're left with just the essence of the present. Some even describe it as a connection to something greater, a sense of unity with the universe.

And hey, let's not forget about dreams! When you're dreaming, time can feel like a wild rollercoaster ride. A minute in the waking world can stretch into hours in a dream. Your consciousness is free to wander, to explore realms where the rules of time don't apply. Ever wake up from a dream and feel like you've lived an entire lifetime in just a few hours? That's the magic of altered states—time becomes fluid, and your consciousness dances freely.

Now, let's shift gears and explore how time perception varies across different psychological states. It's a fascinating landscape, really. Take, for example, when you're in a state of flow—when you're fully engaged in an activity you love. Athletes, artists, and writers often report this experience. It's like being in a time warp; hours can pass in what feels like mere minutes. Your consciousness is so focused, so absorbed, that time becomes a background player, fading into the shadows.

On the other hand, let's consider stress or anxiety. When life feels overwhelming, time can feel like a relentless march forward, each tick of the clock amplifying your worries. You might find yourself checking the time constantly, feeling like the seconds are slipping through your fingers like sand. Your consciousness, in this case, is tethered to the ticking clock, amplifying your sense of urgency and pressure.

So, what's the takeaway from all this? It's clear that our consciousness doesn't just passively experience time; it actively shapes it. By exploring altered states and recognizing how our psychological states influence our perception, we can start to take control.

Imagine if you could harness the power of your consciousness to create a more fulfilling relationship with time. You can! Start small—set aside a few moments each day to simply breathe and be present. Notice how time feels in those moments. Embrace the flow when you're engaged in something you love, and watch how time bends to your will.

As we wrap up this exploration, remember this: time is more than just a ticking clock. It's a dance, a flow, and your consciousness is the lead. Embrace it, explore it, and let it guide you on your journey. You've got this!

Chapter 14

The Role of Time in the Universe

Let's talk about time. It's not just that annoying tick-tock of the clock on the wall or those fleeting moments we try to grab hold of. Nah, time is way deeper than that. It's like this fundamental thread that weaves through the very fabric of the universe. Think of time as the canvas where the universe splashes its wild colors, creating this grand masterpiece we call existence. It's not merely a way to measure life; it's a dimension that shapes everything around us. Without it, the universe would be like a chaotic mess of particles, floating aimlessly in a dark void. But with time? Well, that's where we find rhythm, evolution, and the unfolding tale of everything that is.

So, let's jump into how time plays a role in the evolution of the universe. Picture it: every star that twinkles above, every planet spinning around its sun, every galaxy swirling in the vastness—none of these celestial wonders are just sitting still. They're constantly in motion, grooving to the beat of time. The universe is like a massive symphony, where each note is a moment in time, contributing to the overall melody of creation.

As the universe expands, time stretches right along with it. Remember the Big Bang? That massive explosion of energy and matter kicked off everything we know, marking the beginning of time as we understand it. From that explosive moment onward, time and the cosmos have been intricately linked. It's like a river winding through the landscape of space, carving out valleys and shaping mountains. The universe's evolution? It's all about time, guiding the formation of stars, the birth of galaxies, and the complex dance of celestial mechanics.

But wait—what's in store for the future of time? Now we're getting into some really interesting stuff! Standing on the edge of discovery, the future of time is a tantalizing mystery. The theories of quantum mechanics and relativity are throwing a wrench into our traditional understanding. Could time be more flexible than we ever thought? Can we bend it, twist it, or even travel through it? The answers are lurking in the uncharted waters of scientific exploration.

And here's the kicker: the future of time isn't just some theoretical chatter; it's about how these discoveries could totally change our lives. Imagine a world where we could peek into the future, where the lines between past, present, and future start to blur. What would that mean for our choices, our relationships, and how we see existence? Pretty thrilling, right?

But let's not get ahead of ourselves. As we ponder these possibilities, we gotta remember the responsibility that comes with such knowledge. With great power comes great responsibility, right? The ability to manipulate time could lead to some wild consequences. Just look at all those time travel stories out there—one tiny change can send ripples through reality, altering destinies in ways we can't even wrap our heads around.

So, how do we dance through this intricate relationship between time and the universe? First off, we gotta embrace the idea that time isn't our enemy. It's more like a companion on this crazy journey of life, nudging us to enjoy each moment, learn from the past, and dream about what's next. The universe has its own rhythm, and we're just a part of this cosmic ballet.

To make sense of all this, let's break it down into bite-sized pieces. Here are some key points to keep in mind:

1. Time is a fundamental aspect of the cosmos, shaping the universe and our understanding of existence.

2. The evolution of the universe is intricately tied to the flow of time, guiding the birth and death of celestial bodies.

3. The future of time holds exciting possibilities, but it also comes with responsibility and the potential for unforeseen consequences.

As you mull over these ideas, remember you've got the power to shape your own story within this vast universe. Your experiences, choices, and understanding of time can all influence how you navigate life. Embrace the journey, stay curious, and keep your mind open to the wonders that lie ahead.

In the grand scheme of things, time is a gift. It's the heartbeat of the universe, reminding us to cherish each moment. So, as you think about the role of time in the cosmos, take a moment to appreciate the beauty of your own existence. You're part of this magnificent tapestry, woven together with the threads of time and space.

Now, let's move forward with excitement and anticipation. The universe is waiting, and so are the possibilities that time holds for you. Keep dreaming, keep exploring, and remember: the journey is just as important as the destination. You've got this!

Alright, let's dive deeper into this whole time and universe thing.

Time's been a hot topic for ages. Philosophers, scientists, and even everyday folks have wrestled with its meaning. Some say it's linear—like a straight line stretching from the past to the future. Others argue it's more circular, where everything repeats in cycles. Then there's the idea that time is an illusion, a construct of our minds. Crazy, right? But think about it—how often do we get lost in our thoughts, reminiscing about the past or worrying about the future?

Here's a little anecdote for you: I once sat on a park bench, just watching the world go by. Kids were playing, dogs were barking, and life was happening all around me. For a moment, I felt like I was outside of time. I was just there, soaking it all in. It hit me then—time isn't just something we measure; it's the essence of our experiences. It's how we connect with the world and each other.

Let's chat about how time affects our daily lives. We all live by schedules, right? Work, school, appointments—everything's timed to the minute. But what happens when we step outside of that? When we lose track of time while doing something we love, like painting, playing music, or even just hanging out with friends? Those moments are golden. They remind us that while time can feel constricting, it can also be liberating.

Now, think about how time affects our relationships. Ever notice how some friendships just click, no matter how much time passes? You can go years without seeing someone, but when you finally meet up, it feels like no time has passed at all. It's like time bends around those connections, making them feel timeless. On the flip side, there are those relationships that just fade away. You drift apart, and before you know it, you're strangers. It's a reminder that while time can strengthen bonds, it can also pull them apart.

Speaking of relationships, let's touch on the idea of nostalgia. Isn't it wild how a smell, a song, or a photo can transport you back in time? It's like a little time machine that takes you to moments you thought you'd forgotten. Nostalgia can be bittersweet, can't it? It brings back memories of joy but also reminds us of what we've lost.

Now, let's shift gears and think about time on a grander scale. The universe is constantly changing, right? Stars are born, live their lives, and eventually die, often in spectacular explosions. The life cycle of a star can take millions or even billions of years. When we look up at the night sky, we're not just seeing stars; we're looking back in time. Some of those twinkling lights might be long gone, but their light is still traveling through space, reaching us eons later. Mind-blowing, isn't it?

And what about black holes? These cosmic beasts warp time and space in ways we can barely comprehend. If you were to get close to a black hole, time would slow down for you compared to someone far away. It's like a cosmic trick! The closer you get, the more time stretches. It's a reminder that our perception of time is relative.

Let's also not forget about the ticking clock of our own lives. We're all on borrowed time, really. It's a finite resource, and that can be both freeing and terrifying. Some folks might stress about it, while others might embrace it, living each day to the fullest. It's a personal choice.

In today's fast-paced world, we often rush through life, barely stopping to catch our breath. We're so focused on the next thing—work deadlines, social media updates, that never-ending to-do list—that we forget to just be. But here's the kicker: time isn't just about the future; it's about the now.

Imagine you're at a concert, surrounded by friends, feeling the music pulse through you. That moment? It's all about time. It's about being present, soaking in every beat, every cheer from the crowd. Those are the moments we live for. They remind us that while time keeps moving, we can choose to be fully alive in each second.

Now, let's get back to the universe. It's vast, mysterious, and full of wonders we're only beginning to understand. Scientists are constantly uncovering new truths about time and space, pushing the boundaries of what we know. Just look at how technology has evolved! We're sending probes to distant planets, peering into the depths of black holes, and even trying to unlock the secrets of time travel. It's like we're kids in a cosmic playground, and the universe is our sandbox.

But with all this exploration comes responsibility. As we learn more about time, we have to think about how we use that knowledge. Time travel, for instance—imagine the possibilities! But also the risks. What if we could go back and change something? The ripple effects could be catastrophic. It's a reminder that with great power comes great responsibility.

So, how do we find balance in all this? It starts with mindfulness. Being present in the moment can help us appreciate the beauty of time. Take a walk, breathe in the fresh air, and just be. It's amazing how slowing down can shift our perspective.

And let's not forget the importance of storytelling. Stories are how we make sense of time. They connect our past to our present and future. Think about it— every time you share a memory, you're bending time. You're bringing the past into the now, creating a shared experience. It's a beautiful way to honor the passage of time.

As we wrap this up, let's reflect on what time means to us as individuals. It's a personal journey, after all. We all have our own timelines, our own experiences that shape who we are. Embrace that. Celebrate your journey, the highs and lows, the moments that made you laugh and the ones that brought you to tears.

In the end, time is a gift. It's the heartbeat of the universe, reminding us to cherish each moment. So, as you ponder the role of time in the cosmos, take a moment to appreciate the beauty of your own existence. You're a part of this magnificent tapestry, woven together with the threads of time and space.

Let's move forward with excitement and anticipation. The universe is waiting, and so are the possibilities that time holds for you. Keep dreaming, keep exploring, and remember: the journey is just as important as the destination. You've got this!

Chapter 15

The Future of Time Travel

Picture this: a world where time travel isn't just a crazy fantasy or some wild sci-fi plot twist, but something we can actually do. Pretty wild, right? Just think about the endless possibilities! Let's dive into this intriguing future together.

There's a buzz in the air about what's next in time research. Scientists are on the verge of breakthroughs that could flip our understanding of time upside down. Imagine advanced quantum computers, tapping into the strange world of quantum mechanics, potentially unlocking the secrets to bending time. These machines could help us unravel the complex web of spacetime, stitching together the past, present, and future like a cosmic quilt.

Then there's the mind-blowing idea of wormholes. These theoretical shortcuts through spacetime might just be our golden ticket to time travel. Sure, we're still scratching our heads over the math and physics, but researchers are getting creative, looking into how we might create stable wormholes. If we crack that code, my friend, we could be staring at the front door of a time machine! Just imagine it—hopping through time like it's no big deal.

But wait, there's more! We're also eyeing the role of artificial intelligence in this whole time travel gig. Picture AI systems that can simulate timelines, guiding us through the consequences of our choices before we even make them. It's like having a wise old sage whispering in your ear, helping you dodge the pitfalls of time travel.

Now, let's switch gears for a sec and chat about what time travel could mean for society. It's not just about jumping into a DeLorean or rocking a fancy watch. This could change everything. If time travel becomes a reality, we'll face some serious questions about ethics, responsibility, and the essence of our existence.

Think about it: what if you could zip back and witness key moments in history? The signing of the Declaration of Independence, the first moon landing, or even the dawn of civilization itself. The insights we'd gain from those experiences could totally reshape our view of history and guide our present. But here's the kicker—would we even have the right to change anything?

The implications could ripple through society like a stone thrown into a pond. We'd have to wrestle with causality. Would our actions in the past mess up the future? And if they did, how would we navigate the moral maze of time travel? The weight of that responsibility could be a lot to bear.

Now, let's take a step back and imagine a world where time travel is a thing. Picture a society where folks can explore their ancestry, experiencing their heritage firsthand. Families could gather around the dinner table, swapping stories of their ancestors as if they'd just come back from a trip in time. That kind of connection could build unity and understanding, tearing down walls that divide us.

But it's not just about personal stories. Think of the scientific breakthroughs that could come from this. Researchers could travel back to collect data from the past, observe extinct species in their natural habitats, or study climate change over centuries. The knowledge we could gather would be priceless, shaping policies and practices for a healthier planet.

And let's not forget the entertainment side of things! Time travel could totally change how we experience stories. Imagine immersive experiences where you could step into a historical event, feeling the weight of the moment. It'd be like living in a novel, with you as the main character, crafting your own adventure.

But as we dream about this future, we've gotta be careful. The allure of time travel comes with a hefty dose of responsibility. We need to approach this frontier with respect, knowing that with great power comes great responsibility. The choices we make could echo through time, shaping destinies we can't even begin to imagine.

So, as we stand on the edge of possibility, let's keep our eyes peeled. The future of time travel isn't just a scientific quest; it's a philosophical journey. It pushes us to rethink our relationship with time, history, and each other.

You, my friend, have a role in this unfolding story. Whether you're a scientist, a dreamer, or just someone curious about the universe's mysteries, your voice counts. Engage with these ideas, ponder the implications, and join the conversation.

Remember, the journey of a thousand miles starts with a single step. We might not have all the answers today, but just thinking about these questions is a step toward a brighter, more connected future.

So, let's dream big, explore the unknown, and embrace the adventure ahead. Time travel might be just around the corner, and who knows? You could be one of the pioneers blazing the trail.

In this grand tapestry of existence, your story is woven into the fabric of time. Embrace it, cherish it, and let's see where this journey takes us!

Now, let's dig deeper into some of these concepts. Time travel isn't just a one-way street; it's a winding road with twists and turns. You've got to think about the mechanics behind it. If we're talking wormholes, we're diving into some serious physics. Einstein's theory of relativity hints at the possibility of warping spacetime. It's like bending a piece of paper to bring two points closer together. But the science is complicated.

Creating a stable wormhole? That's no small feat. We're talking about exotic matter, negative energy, and all sorts of wild theories. It's like trying to build a bridge with spaghetti—sounds fun, but is it really gonna hold up?

And then there's the whole question of paradoxes. You've heard of the grandfather paradox, right? If you go back in time and accidentally stop your grandfather from meeting your grandmother, do you even exist? Mind-bending stuff! These paradoxes could throw a wrench in the gears of time travel.

So, how do we handle that? Well, some scientists suggest the idea of multiverses. You know, like a cosmic game of "what if." Every time you make a choice, a new universe branches off. So, if you went back and changed something, you wouldn't erase your own existence; you'd just create a new timeline.

But, hey, that opens up a whole new can of worms. If we can create alternate timelines, what happens to our original one? Are we just hopping from one reality to another, leaving a trail of chaos behind us? That's a slippery slope, my friend.

And let's talk about the ethics of it all. If time travel becomes a reality, who gets to decide what's right or wrong? Should we intervene in historical events? It's like playing god. Some folks might want to prevent wars or disasters, while others might just want to see how things play out.

Imagine the debates! You'd have historians, ethicists, and everyday folks all weighing in. It could turn into a heated discussion—like a family arguing over the best pizza toppings. Everyone's got their opinion, and nobody's backing down.

But what if we could use time travel for good? Picture this: we could send scientists back to gather data on climate change, see how ecosystems reacted in the past, and use that knowledge to make better decisions today. It's like having a cheat sheet for the future.

Or think about education. Students could take field trips to ancient Rome or the Renaissance. Learning history would be way cooler when you're actually there, soaking it all in. It'd be like a real-life history lesson, and who wouldn't want that?

And let's not forget the potential for healing. Imagine being able to revisit moments of personal loss or trauma, gaining closure in a way we never thought possible. It could be a powerful tool for mental health, allowing people to confront their pasts in a safe way.

But, of course, there's the flip side. What if people misuse time travel? The potential for abuse is huge. You could have folks trying to profit from past events or even worse—trying to erase mistakes. It's a slippery slope, and we'd need some serious safeguards in place.

So, what's the takeaway here? Time travel is a fascinating concept, filled with possibilities and pitfalls. It's not just about the science; it's about how we navigate the moral landscape that comes with it.

As we look ahead, let's keep the conversation going. The future of time travel is a shared journey, and we all have a part to play. Whether you're a scientist, a dreamer, or just someone who loves a good story, your thoughts matter.

Let's keep dreaming big and exploring the unknown. Time travel might just be waiting for us around the corner, and who knows what adventures await?

In this grand tapestry of existence, your story is woven into the fabric of time. Embrace it, cherish it, and let's see where this journey takes us!

Index

www.ingramcontent.com/pod-product-compliance
Lightning Source LLC
Chambersburg PA
CBHW022135150726

47992CB00002B/617